Nothing Needs to be Fixed

By: Trent Goodbaudy

Trent Goodbaudy

Copyright © 2026 Trent Goodbaudy
All rights reserved.
ISBN: 9798243234979

Table of Contents

Opening Page 1
PART I — WHEN SOMETHING TOOK OVER 3
   When Something Else Started Holding You.............................5
   How Control Became Safer Than Feeling 9
   Why Trying Harder Never Solved It...13
PART II — WHEN THE SELF STEPPED BACK 17
   The Moment You Stopped Trusting Yourself 19
   When the Habit Became the Boss...23
   How a Label Can Feel Like Shelter 27
PART III — WHY MOST SOLUTIONS DON'T LAST 31
   The Trap of Always Watching Yourself...................................33
   When One Habit Becomes Another..37
   When Belonging Replaces Trust..41
PART IV — WHEN THINGS START TO SETTLE 45
   The Return of Your Own Signals 47
   When the Habit Is No Longer Needed.....................................51
   The Calm That Isn't Empty 55
PART V — LIFE WITHOUT THE FIGHT 59
   Why You Don't Miss It 61
   Living Without Watching Yourself 65
   When Nothing Needs to Be Said 69
   End Page 73
   About the Author 75

Trent Goodbaudy

For my daughter.

Trent Goodbaudy

Opening Page

You don't have to change anything to read this book.

You don't have to agree with it.
You don't have to do anything with it.

These pages are not here to fix you
or ask you to become someone else.

They are here to offer a little quiet
in a world that is often too loud.

You can read slowly.
You can stop at any time.
You can close the book and come back later.

Nothing is required.

Trent Goodbaudy

PART I — WHEN SOMETHING TOOK OVER

Trent Goodbaudy

1

When Something Else Started Holding You

Addiction didn't begin with a substance.
It began when something inside you got tired.

Most people think addiction starts when someone takes a drug, pours a drink, or does a thing too often.
But that is not where it really begins.

It begins when life becomes too loud, too sharp, or too heavy to carry the way you used to.

Something inside you tries to keep up.
It tries to stay strong.
It tries to keep going.

And at some point, it gets tired.

When that happens, something else steps in.

Maybe it was a pill.
Maybe it was a drink.
Maybe it was a screen, a needle, a rush, or a habit.

Whatever it was, it did not arrive as a problem.

It arrived as **relief**.

It made the noise fade.
It softened the edges.
It made things feel quieter inside.

For a moment, you could breathe again.

That is why it stayed.

People do not keep doing things that only hurt them.
They keep doing things that once helped them.

The behavior gave you a place to rest.
It gave you something to lean on.
It helped you get through what felt too much.

That does not make you weak.
It means something in you was still trying to survive.

Over time, the thing that helped started to hurt.
It began to take more than it gave.
But by then, it had already become part of how you stayed upright.

Not because you loved it.
But because you needed what it gave.

This is not a story about bad choices.
It is a story about something that stepped in when something else could not hold you anymore.

And for a while, it worked.

Signals

- The behavior felt like relief before it felt like trouble
- It made things quieter
- It helped you keep going

Quiet Page

You didn't reach for it because you were broken.
You reached for it because something was hurting.

For a moment, it helped you stand.

You don't have to be ashamed of wanting the pain to stop.

Let it be quiet here.

2

How Control Became Safer Than Feeling

When your own signals stop feeling safe, something else steps in.

There was a time when you could feel what you needed.
When to rest.
When to move.
When to stop.

But when life becomes overwhelming, those signals can start to feel wrong.

You don't know when to pause.
You don't know what you're feeling.
You don't know what will happen next.

Everything feels loose.

So something tighter takes over.

A habit.
A substance.
A pattern.

It begins to tell you when you feel okay.
When you can relax.
When the day is over.

It gives you edges.

Even if those edges hurt, they feel safer than falling.

Without it, things feel wide and unclear.
With it, there is at least a rule.

You don't have to guess anymore.
You don't have to listen inside.
You just follow what the habit says.

That is why control can feel like safety.

Not because it is kind.
But because it is certain.

When your own feelings don't feel safe to trust,
something that gives clear limits can feel like relief.

Even if it costs you.

Signals

- The habit told you when to rest or feel
- Without it, things felt loose or scary
- Control felt better than not knowing

Quiet Page

When the inside feels unsure,
something firm can feel like shelter.

It doesn't mean you wanted to be trapped.
It means you wanted to feel held.

You don't have to decide anything right now.
Just notice how it feels to be here.

3

Why Trying Harder Never Solved It

Fighting the habit only made it louder.

Most people think the answer is to try harder.
To be stronger.
To push back.

But something strange happens when you fight a habit.

You end up thinking about it more.
Watching it more.
Bracing against it.

The thing you are trying to get away from
starts to take up even more space.

Willpower feels like it should work.
But it often just makes you tired.

You hold your breath.
You clench.
You wait.

And when the grip slips,
the relief feels even stronger than before.

Not because you failed.
But because you were exhausted.

The habit didn't get louder because you are weak.
It got louder because you were pushing on it.

The more you struggle,
the more the struggle becomes the center of everything.

That's not freedom.
That's just another way of being trapped.

Signals

- Pushing it away made it stronger
- Willpower made you tired
- Relief came back fast

Quiet Page

You were not losing a battle.
You were getting worn out.

Sometimes what sounds like strength
is just pain holding its breath.

You don't have to fight anything here.
You can let the noise settle.

PART II — WHEN THE SELF STEPPED BACK

Trent Goodbaudy

4

The Moment You Stopped Trusting Yourself

Something happened that made your own timing feel unsafe.

There was a time when you knew what you wanted.
Not in a big way.
Just enough to get through the day.

You knew when you were hungry.
When you were tired.
When something felt right or wrong.

But when things become painful or confusing, that sense can fade.

You start to second-guess yourself.
You don't know what you feel.
You don't know what to do next.

Even simple choices feel risky.

So you begin to look outside yourself.

Other people.
Other rules.
Other things.

You want something to tell you when it's okay.
When to move.
When to stop.

Waiting starts to feel dangerous.
Silence feels loud.
Not knowing feels unbearable.

So you reach for something that answers for you.

Not because you wanted to give up control,
but because you didn't feel safe having it.

Signals

- You stopped knowing what you wanted
- You looked outside yourself for answers
- Waiting felt dangerous

Quiet Page

When your own voice goes quiet,
the world starts to sound very loud.

It's not wrong to want something to guide you.
It just means you didn't feel safe being alone inside.

You can rest here for a moment.

Trent Goodbaudy

5

When the Habit Became the Boss

The behavior started running things.

At first, the habit was something you used.
Something you reached for.

But over time, it began to do more than help.
It began to decide.

It told you when you felt okay.
When the day was bearable.
When you could finally relax.

It started to set the pace.

When to wake up.
When to stop.
When you were allowed to feel calm.

You didn't have to guess anymore.
The habit gave you rules.

And rules can feel safe
when everything else feels uncertain.

Even if the rules are harsh,
they are clear.

So the habit took on a role
your own sense of timing used to hold.

Not because you wanted to be ruled,
but because being lost felt worse.

Signals

- It decided when you felt okay
- It told you when to stop or start
- It gave you rules

Quiet Page

When life feels unsteady,
even a hard rule can feel like a handrail.

You didn't choose to be controlled.
You chose to feel steady.

You don't have to let go of anything right now.
Just notice how it feels to stand here.

Trent Goodbaudy

6

How a Label Can Feel Like Shelter

Sometimes "this is who I am" feels safer than not knowing.

When things feel unclear inside,
a name can feel like a place to stand.

"I'm an addict."
"I'm broken."
"This is just who I am."

A label gives shape to the pain.
It tells you where you fit.
It gives you something to hold.

Without it, everything feels wide and uncertain.
With it, at least you know where you are.

Even if the label hurts,
it can feel safer than being lost.

Letting go of it feels like stepping into open space.
You don't know what will catch you.
You don't know who you'll be.

So the label becomes a kind of shelter.
Not because it's kind,
but because it's familiar.

Signals

- The label gave you a place to stand
- Letting go of it felt scary
- Being free felt risky

Quiet Page

Names can feel like walls.
They hold you in place.

You don't have to tear anything down.
Just notice how it feels
to imagine a little more room.

PART III — WHY MOST SOLUTIONS DON'T LAST

7

The Trap of Always Watching Yourself

If you always have to guard something, it isn't really gone.

When a habit becomes the center of your life,
even trying to stop it can keep it in control.

You start watching yourself.

Did I think about it?
Did I want it?
Am I okay right now?

Your mind stays on alert.
Your body stays tight.

Fear never really leaves.
You are always waiting for something to go wrong.

Even when nothing is happening,
you're still checking.

That's not peace.
That's just a different kind of tension.

You may not be using,
but the habit is still close.

Not because it is strong,
but because it is being watched.

Signals

- Fear never leaves
- You never relax
- You're always checking

Quiet Page

A guard never gets to rest.

If you've been watching yourself for a long time,
you might be very tired.

You don't have to stay on alert here.
Nothing is being tested.

8

When One Habit Becomes Another

Sometimes control just changes shape.

When one habit leaves,
another can quietly take its place.

It might look better from the outside.
Healthier.
More acceptable.

But inside, the feeling is the same.

You become strict.
You make rules.
You hold yourself tight.

You trade one thing for another.
The object changes,
but the pressure does not.

You still feel tense.
You still feel watched.
You still feel like you have to manage yourself.

That's not freedom.
That's just a new way of holding on.

Signals

- You get strict instead of free
- You trade one thing for another
- You still feel tense

Quiet Page

Changing the shape of a cage
does not make it disappear.

You don't have to build anything new here.
You can let the grip soften.

9
When Belonging Replaces Trust

Sometimes groups feel safer than being on your own.

When you don't trust yourself,
being with others can feel like a lifeline.

They tell you who you are.
They tell you what to do.
They tell you when you're okay.

It feels good not to have to decide.

But over time, something shifts.

You start to feel lost without them.
You worry about leaving.
You change yourself to fit in.

Belonging becomes another way of staying safe.

Not because you are weak,
but because being alone inside feels scary.

So you stay close.
You listen.
You adjust.

And your own voice gets quieter.

Signals

- You feel lost without them
- You worry about leaving
- You change to fit in

Quiet Page

It's natural to want to be held by others.
No one is meant to do everything alone.

Just notice how it feels
to listen for your own voice again.

PART IV — WHEN THINGS START TO SETTLE

Trent Goodbaudy

10

The Return of Your Own Signals

You begin to feel what's right again.

At some point, something shifts.

You don't have to push as much.
You don't have to hold so tight.

You start to notice small things.

When you're tired.
When you're full.
When something feels enough.

The cravings don't shout the way they used to.
They come and go.
They don't take over.

You don't have to force yourself anymore.
Choices feel lighter.
You can wait.

Waiting no longer feels dangerous.
It just feels like time passing.

And in that space,
your own sense of what's right
starts to come back.

Signals

- Cravings feel quieter
- You don't have to force yourself
- Waiting feels okay

Quiet Page

When the noise fades,
something gentle can be heard.

It doesn't rush.
It doesn't shout.

You don't have to grab it.
Just let it be here.

11

When the Habit Is No Longer Needed

It fades because there is nothing for it to do.

Something simple begins to happen.

The habit shows up less.
Not because you pushed it away,
but because it has nothing to fix.

You don't fight it.
You don't argue with it.
You don't even think about it much.

It just... doesn't come.

The space it used to fill
is already full of something quieter.

You are not holding yourself together anymore.
You are just here.

And when nothing is broken,
nothing has to step in.

Signals

- It doesn't show up
- You don't fight it
- You don't think about it

Quiet Page

When something has no job,
it can rest.

You don't have to make anything leave.
You can let it notice
it is no longer needed.

Trent Goodbaudy

12

The Calm That Isn't Empty

Nothing needs to fill the space.

When the noise is gone,
you might expect a hole.

But what you find instead
is something quiet and steady.

You don't need to replace anything.
You don't need a new habit.
You don't need a new rule.

You just feel here.

There is nothing pulling at you.
Nothing pushing you.

Life feels simple in a way
that is hard to explain.

Not exciting.
Not dull.

Just enough.

Signals

- You don't need to replace anything
- You just feel here
- Life feels simple

Quiet Page

This quiet is not empty.
It is full of you.

You don't have to fill it.
You can let it hold you.

Trent Goodbaudy

PART V — LIFE WITHOUT THE FIGHT

Trent Goodbaudy

13

Why You Don't Miss It

There is no drama when something is done.

When something truly ends,
it doesn't leave a loud space behind.

You don't look back.
You don't feel sad.
You don't feel proud.

It's just over.

Not in a big way.
Not in a story you tell.

It simply stops being part of your life.

You don't wonder about it.
You don't argue with it.
You don't wish for it.

You move on without noticing you did.

Signals

- You don't look back
- You don't feel sad
- You don't feel proud

Quiet Page

Some things don't end with fireworks.
They end with silence.

That silence is not loss.
It is peace.

14

Living Without Watching Yourself

You don't have to keep track anymore.

There was a time when you checked yourself all day.

Am I okay?
Did I think about it?
Did I want it?

Now, you forget to check.

Not because you are trying,
but because there is nothing to watch.

Time feels normal again.
Days pass.
Nights come and go.

You live your life.

Not as someone in recovery.
Not as someone in danger.

Just as someone here.

Signals

- You forget to check
- Time feels normal
- You live your life

Quiet Page

You were never meant
to be your own guard.

You can rest now.
Life will hold you.

Trent Goodbaudy

15

When Nothing Needs to Be Said

Silence means things are okay.

When something no longer runs your life,
you stop talking about it.

You don't explain.
You don't tell the story.
You don't go over the past.

It just fades into the background.

The story falls away.

Not because it was wrong,
but because it is no longer needed.

You don't have to be someone who survived something.
You don't have to be someone who overcame.

You just are.

Signals

- You don't explain
- The story falls away
- You just are

Quiet Page

You don't have to prove anything.

You don't have to remember who you were.

You are here.
That is enough.

End Page

You don't need to hold onto anything here.

Nothing is being asked of you.
Nothing is being taken from you.

Whatever brought you this far
can rest.

There is no next step.
There is no right way to feel.

Just this quiet.

Let it be.

About the Author

The author wrote this book because someone he loved did not survive the moment when pain became too heavy to carry alone.

He does not share that story for sympathy, and he does not offer this book as a promise. It is simply the truth that shaped these pages. When you have watched someone you love disappear into a world that felt unbearable to them, you learn how quiet suffering can be, and how easily it can be misunderstood.

This book was written to remove a small part of that misunderstanding.

Rather than asking people to fight themselves, to be fixed, or to be reshaped, the author wanted to create something that could sit with a person in pain without judgment. Something that could offer space instead of pressure. Something that could make it a little easier to stay.

There is no program here, no system to follow, and no role to perform. Just a way of seeing that leaves people a little less alone with what they are carrying.

That is the intention behind this book.

Trent Goodbaudy

About LibertyTruth.org

Beyond books, LibertyTruth.org offers additional writing, tools, and projects for readers interested in sustained clarity rather than momentary insight. Nothing here promises transformation. Nothing claims to replace your judgment.

The goal is simpler—and harder.

To help you see what you may already be living inside, so that whatever choices follow are genuinely your own.

Visit **LibertyTruth.org** if you want to continue exploring this work—quietly, independently, and without instruction.

Made in the USA
Coppell, TX
22 February 2026

72089060R10046